BIG

Elephants

Shelby Braidich

Rosen
REAL
READERS

The Rosen Publishing Group, Inc.
New York

Elephants are the biggest animals that live on land.

Most elephants are gray.

Elephants have long trunks.

Elephants have white tusks.

4

Elephants eat a lot of food every day.

Some elephants live in zoos.

A baby elephant is called a calf.

Words to Know

calf

elephant

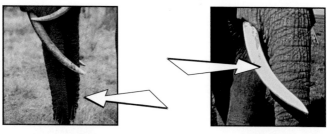

trunk

tusk